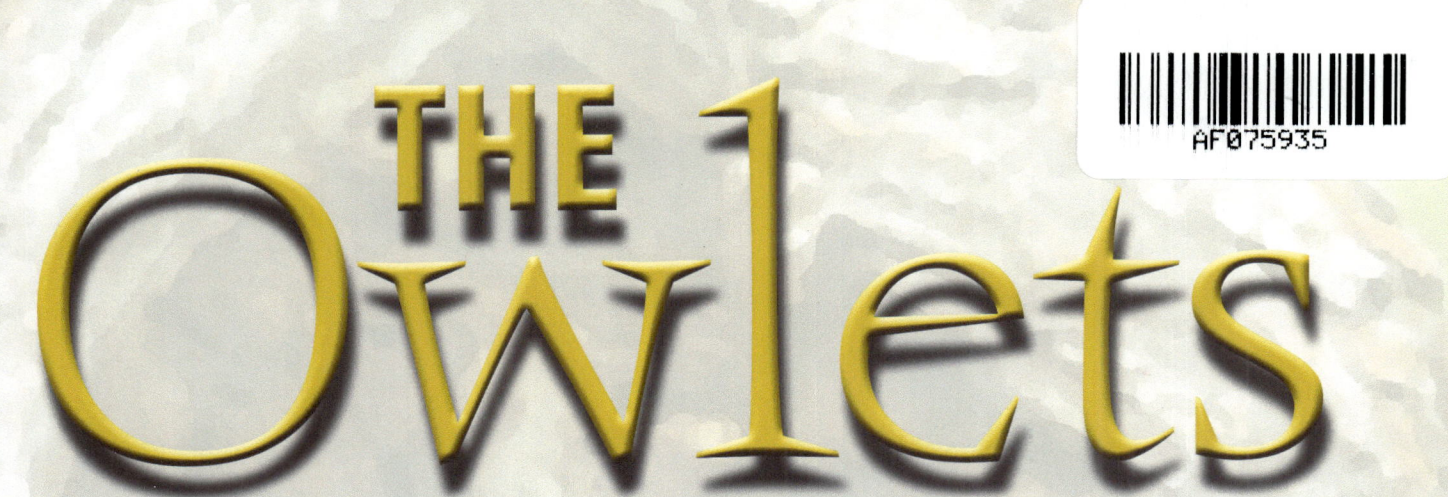

THE Owlets

Written by Ethel "Granny" Franks

Copyright © 2014 by Ethel Franks
All rights reserved. Published by the Peppertree Press, LLC.
the Peppertree Press and associated logos are trademarks of the Peppertree Press, LLC.

No part of this publication may be reproduced, stored in a retrieval system, transmitted in any form or by any means, electronic, mechanical, photocopying, recording, or otherwise, without prior written permission of the publisher and author/illustrator.

Owlette photography: Tom Spada

Designed by Parry Design Studio, Inc.

For information regarding permissions, call 941.922.2662
or contact us at our website:
www.peppertreepublishing.com or write to:
the Peppertree Press, LLC.,
Attention: Publisher
1269 First Street, Suite 7
Sarasota, Florida 34236

ISBN: 978-1-61493-281-9
Library of Congress Control Number: 2014909881
Printed in the U.S.A.

Printed (June, 2014)

Olivia, a Great Horned Owl, was very excited! She knew that very soon she would lay her eggs and after they hatched she would be a mother to baby owls.

After she thought about the coming event, she wondered, "Where will we live? The trees nearby were perfect for a nest - but - the streets were really, really noisy." Since she lived near the railroad tracks the air was often filled with smoke and soot. Not a great place for new little owls.

"What to do? What to do?"

Then Olivia had a sudden thought.
Why couldn't she, the expected babies and their daddy (Oscar), all fly to a better place to live and raise their babies?
What a great idea!

When Olivia told Oscar about her big plan, he asked,
"Just where do you think we can go?"

"Well," replied Olivia, "Maybe a place that is not so noisy, where the air is clean and it's warmer.
What do you think of my idea?"

"It sounds okay," said Oscar. "I guess we'll need to head south."

When their friend, Rita the Robin, heard of their plans she was very upset. She cried, "Please, please don't go away! Don't leave me!"

"No problem," remarked Olivia, "You can come with us. Wouldn't that be fun?"

Sadly, Rita the Robin said, "Oh, I'd love to go with you, but remember that we're in Michigan and since I'm the State Bird, I really need to stay here. I'll miss you so much!"

The next morning Olivia headed south with Oscar following closely to keep an eye on her, making sure she was safe.

After Olivia had flown many miles she landed in a big tree. She noticed a pretty red bird perched on a nearby branch.

"Hi there," called Olivia. "My name is Olivia. I'm flying south – looking for a good place to raise my family. I'm an owl. What kind of bird are you?"

"Hi, Olivia! I'm Cathy," replied the red bird. "I don't know where you're from but you're in Indiana now. I'm a cardinal and live here all the time. The weather is usually nice, but it gets cold here and often snows. How long will you be staying?"

"We'll spend the night here and then keep moving. Why don't you come with us? It could be a real adventure!"

"Oh, goodness, no. I can't do that. I have to stay in Indiana. I'm the State Bird. You probably should know that if you go through Ohio, Illinois, Kentucky, North Carolina, Virginia or West Virginia, the Cardinal (like myself) is also their State Bird, so they couldn't join you either," answered Cathy

As they continued their journey, Olivia thought she should have asked Cathy that since Rhode Island is the smallest state, could the hummingbird be that state's bird?
I'll have to find out."

After the owls had flown many miles Olivia wondered, "Where are we?" she called to Oscar and asked if he knew. Oscar said he'd just seen a sign for Florida and later a smaller sign that showed QUAIL'S RUN. The sign had some type of birds on it. He wondered if the quail might be Florida's state bird.

Olivia didn't have an answer for that but knew she needed rest.

Oscar spied a big tree with sturdy branches with moss hanging down. He shouted, "That tree looks perfect for us! Let's stop here."

A short while after they found the tree, Oscar had the nest ready because he had heard Olivia say, "Oh, my, oh my! I think it's time to lay my eggs."

It seemed like forever before the eggs hatched, but then Olivia and Oscar had two adorable owlets.

"Oh, how precious." thought Olivia. "I'll take such good care of you. We'll be so happy here. Maye we'll meet some of those quails and have them as friends."

The next morning, Olivia and her tiny babies awoke to see a group of people standing below their tree, pointing up at them, laughing and shouting to each other. "Look up! See the baby owls?"

Olivia was thrilled to hear all the friendly voices. She knew they were admiring her new babies. Olivia was so excited she started flapping her wings. As she turned, one of her wings caught little Angie Owlet and tipped her out of the tree.

The crowd below gasped and shouted, "Oh no!" Olivia was so frightened. "What would happen to her baby? Is she hurt? Would those people hurt her or steal her? Oh, what to do?"

Then Oscar came swooping over to the tree shouting. "Oscar, Jr., did you push little Angie out of the nest? I hope she's alright!"

Olivia quickly exclaimed, "No, no, it was my fault. It was an accident, but she's okay. I hear her peeping."

As they looked down, they saw a white-haired man tenderly pick up the tiny owl. "Oh no, oh no, please, please," cried Olivia. "Leave her alone, don't hurt my baby!"

But the old man didn't put her down. He tucked the tiny owl in his shirt pocket and started climbing the tree. The hushed crowd watched as he reached the nest and carefully placed the tiny owl in it. Then he slowly climbed back down the tree.

All the people watching started clapping and cheering!

Olivia's next thought was "Quail or no quail here – we're staying... it's a wonderful place to be."

These pictures inspired this story of the Owlets.

This story was written with fond memories of Grandpa Keith and the years past when we wrote stories for our loving grandchildren.

Granny's ideas paired with Grandpa's editing and typing in those good old days – A cherished time together.

State Bird Map

www.ingramcontent.com/pod-product-compliance
Ingram Content Group UK Ltd.
Pitfield, Milton Keynes, MK11 3LW, UK
UKHW060132240426
12048UKWH00002B/3